i

Department of Defense Strategy for Countering Weapons of Mass Destruction

JUNE 2014

CONTENTS

SECRETARY'S FOREWORD

The pursuit of weapons of mass destruction (WMD) and potential use by actors of concern pose a threat to U.S. national security and peace and stability around the world. Adversaries may use WMD to threaten or carry out attacks on the United States, our forces at home or abroad, or our allies and partners. Our political will and military capability to provide security, resist coercion, and defeat aggression must not be undermined by WMD.

This document, the Department of Defense Strategy for Countering Weapons of Mass Destruction, represents the Department of Defense's response to the WMD threat. It specifies desired end states, prescribes priority objectives, delineates a strategic approach for achieving those objectives, and outlines the countering WMD activities and tasks necessary for success.

In a constrained fiscal environment, we are focusing our efforts on preventing acquisition and countering the most likely threats. Accordingly, this strategy emphasizes early action through pathway defeat, shaping the environment to dissuade actors from pursuing WMD, and cooperating with partners to achieve countering WMD goals. We are prioritizing capabilities that counter operationally significant risks and activities that are best executed by the Department rather than by partners in the U.S. Government or the international community.

This strategy provides foundational guidance for enacting the Department's countering WMD policies, plans, and programs and advances a comprehensive response to existing and developing WMD threats.

Chuck Hagel
Secretary of Defense

MEMORANDUM FOR SECRETARIES OF THE MILITARY DEPARTMENTS
                UNDER SECRETARIES OF DEFENSE
                DEPUTY CHIEF MANAGEMENT OFFICER
                CHIEFS OF THE MILITARY SERVICES
                COMMANDERS OF THE COMBATANT COMMANDS
                DIRECTORS OF THE DEFENSE AGENCIES
                DIRECTORS OF THE DOD FIELD ACTIVITIES
                DIRECTORS OF THE JOINT STAFF DIRECTORATES

SUBJECT: Endorsement of Department of Defense Strategy for Countering Weapons of Mass
         Destruction

1. The United States faces threats from state and non-state actors that seek to develop,
proliferate, acquire, or use weapons of mass destruction (WMD). The goal of this strategy is to
ensure the United States and its allies and partners are not attacked or coerced by adversaries
possessing WMD.

2. The military will pursue the three counter-WMD ends defined in the Department of Defense
Strategy for Countering Weapons of Mass Destruction (DoDS-CWMD) to ensure that no new
actors obtain WMD, those possessing WMD do not use them, and—if WMD are used—their
effects are minimized. We will advance these ends through the four priority objectives while
continuously preparing the Department's capabilities in support of the CWMD lines of effort:
preventing acquisition, containing and reducing threats, and responding to crises.

3. The strategy draws on recent experiences and lessons learned since the National Military
Strategy to Combat Weapons of Mass Destruction (NMS-CWMD) was published on
13 February 2006. In light of the progress achieved since then and the integration of key aspects
of the NMS-CWMD, I rescind it upon publication of the DoDS-CWMD.

4. I endorse the DoDS-CWMD. Our capability to defeat aggression will not be undermined by
the threatened or actual use of WMD.

MARTIN E. DEMPSEY
General, U.S. Army

Executive Summary

Potential adversaries of the United States continue to pursue weapons of mass destruction (WMD) to enhance their international influence and achieve greater strategic leverage against U.S. advantages. Increased access to expertise, materials, and technologies heightens the risk that these adversaries will seek, acquire, proliferate, and employ WMD. Furthermore, instability in states pursuing or possessing WMD or related capabilities could lead to dangerous WMD crises.

The Department of Defense Strategy for Countering Weapons of Mass Destruction seeks to ensure that the United States and its allies and partners are neither attacked nor coerced by actors with WMD. It outlines three end states: no new WMD possession, no WMD use, and minimization of WMD effects. The strategy also establishes countering WMD priority objectives for the Department of Defense (DoD), defines an approach for achieving them, and identifies essential activities and tasks.

Countering WMD (CWMD) objectives focus on cooperative efforts to shape the security environment and take early action against adversaries. These objectives are to reduce incentives to pursue, possess, and employ WMD; to increase the barriers to WMD acquisition, proliferation, and use; to manage WMD risks emanating from hostile, fragile, or failed states and safe havens; and to deny the effects of current and emerging WMD threats through layered, integrated defenses.

These objectives are advanced through three lines of effort: Prevent Acquisition, Contain and Reduce Threats, and Respond to Crises. These are supported by a strategic enabler, Prepare—the continuous cycle of ensuring that the Department's capabilities support essential CWMD activities, including maintaining and expanding technical expertise. This approach represents the full range of efforts undertaken by DoD to counter WMD risks.

To implement this approach, the Department engages in activities to understand the environment, threats, and vulnerabilities; control, defeat, disable, and dispose of WMD threats; and safeguard the force and manage WMD consequences. These activities require combining enabling capabilities with specialized CWMD capabilities to address specific threats. DoD prioritizes capabilities that counter operationally significant risks and that are not available elsewhere in the U.S. Government.

The Department incorporates its CWMD efforts into broader plans and operations within DoD, across the U.S. Government, and with international partners. DoD will continue to support CWMD efforts for which other agencies and departments have lead responsibilities.

INTRODUCTION

Actors of concern pose a threat of developing, acquiring, proliferating, or employing weapons of mass destruction (WMD) and related capabilities—expertise, materials, technologies, and means of delivery. These activities present a clear threat to the strategic objectives of the United States. State or non-state actors may use WMD to conduct a catastrophic attack on U.S. citizens and infrastructure; to exploit U.S. power projection, sustainment, and force protection vulnerabilities; to deny access to an area or region and limit the ability of the United States to respond to urgent threats; or to undermine the support for U.S. policies and actions by key regional partners.

This strategy seeks to ensure that the United States and its allies and partners are neither attacked nor coerced by actors with WMD. It delineates three end states: that no new actors obtain WMD, those possessing WMD do not use them, and if actors use WMD, their effects are minimized. It is imperative that our political will and military capability to provide security, resist coercion, and defeat aggression are not undermined by the threatened or actual use of WMD. As part of a whole-of-government effort, the Department of Defense (DoD) will continue to build new capabilities, coalitions, mechanisms, and international norms in cooperation with allies and partners to counter WMD.

Countering WMD (CWMD) consists of efforts against actors of concern to curtail the conceptualization, development, possession, proliferation, use, and effects of WMD and related capabilities. These efforts emphasize shaping the security environment to influence state and non-state actors to eschew WMD-related activities. They focus on addressing WMD developments as early as possible and protecting the force against operationally significant threats. DoD will closely integrate these efforts into broader plans and operations.

This strategy reflects the contemporary and emerging WMD challenge and provides a strong foundation for developing and implementing necessary policies, plans, and programs.

THE WMD CHALLENGE

The pursuit of WMD and the risk of employment by actors of concern pose a persistent threat to peace and stability worldwide and to the national security objectives of the United States. State and non-state actors can use licit and illicit networks and exploit political instability and security gaps to develop, acquire, and proliferate WMD and related capabilities. Due to continuing advances in technology, these WMD threats are likely to become more difficult to identify and defend against. They are an enduring feature of the security environment.

Acquisition Incentives

Acquisition incentives vary depending on an actor's relative global, regional, and domestic positions and circumstances. Actors of concern seek the means to counter rivals' military and technological advantages or hold their interests at risk. They believe possessing WMD will result in enhanced strategic leverage; greater means for coercion; and the capability to deter, disrupt, or defeat military operations or cause mass casualty attacks. Other important motivations include prestige, ideology, regional rivalries, regime-change pressures, and domestic instability. Some actors may opportunistically exploit circumstances to acquire WMD or material of concern—weapons-usable chemical, biological, radiological, or nuclear (CBRN) material in sufficient quantities to produce WMD or critical components. Actors pursuing or possessing WMD often challenge global norms, regional balances of power, and U.S. objectives. These actions make conflict more likely in key regions, heighten the effects of local or regional crises, and create new acquisition incentives through cascading effects.

Adversaries actively seeking or already possessing WMD present a significant intelligence and defense planning challenge. Their strategic intentions, decision-making procedures, and capabilities may be difficult to assess and influence. They may exhibit risk-taking behaviors and be unreceptive to U.S. strategic messaging, challenging our ability to dissuade pursuit and possession and deter use. Some adversaries provide support—including WMD and related capabilities—to other governments and non-state actors. These recipients may employ WMD independently or as proxies. Military campaigns face greater challenges if an adversary is prepared to employ WMD to raise the costs of achieving operational and strategic objectives. An adversary could seek to leverage WMD in a number of ways to shape the course of events at the strategic, operational, and tactical levels (e.g., to attack the U.S. homeland, deter or respond to U.S. engagement, weaken an international coalition, disrupt combat operations, or deny terrain).

WMD Pathways

A wider range of actors can now create and access new and more sophisticated WMD pathways due to the increased flow of expertise and illicit, dual-use, and non-controlled items through trans-regional connections. WMD pathways consist of networks (links among individuals, groups, organizations, governmental entities, etc.) that enable actors to conceptualize, develop, possess, and proliferate WMD and related capabilities. These networks encompass ideas, materials, technologies, facilities, processes, products, and events. Pathways can lower barriers to acquisition and often challenge efforts to detect, identify, and respond to pursuit attempts, especially those shielded by legitimate activities such as CBRN defense programs.

Identifying and disrupting WMD pathways depends on understanding the relations among actors of concern and their supporting networks. It is often difficult to monitor WMD programs due to the wide range of supporting items and personnel. Efforts must distinguish between licit and illicit activities and track the transit of goods and people across regions to reveal networks. Additionally, the need to conduct predictive threat analysis will place ever-growing demands on intelligence and other capabilities. Consequently, efforts to maintain situational awareness and forecast WMD threats will continue to be a challenge.

Vulnerable, Lost, or Stolen WMD

Both state and non-state actors interested in WMD could seek to exploit fragile or failed states with WMD programs or related capabilities. Despite significant progress in securing vulnerable WMD materials, new avenues for exploitation continuously emerge. These developments contribute to the risk of dangerous WMD crises involving the theft or loss of control of weapons or material of concern. These crises could lead to acquisition by hostile actors.

Proliferation risks also arise from the potential convergence of violent extremism, political instability, and inadequate WMD security. Highly motivated non-state actors determined to obtain and employ WMD pose an exceptional risk because they are difficult to dissuade and deter. It is essential to deny them access to all sources of WMD capabilities. Violent extremists are also expanding their geographic reach into ungoverned spaces that could be used to support illicit activities, including development and proliferation of WMD-related capabilities. These safe havens enhance adversaries' freedom of action.

Advances in WMD

The constant evolution of weapons, materials, and technologies makes dissuasion, detection, deterrence, and defense more difficult. Challenges may also arise from innovative concepts of operation or sustained employment of existing WMD technologies. Nuclear weapons remain a prominent concern. The spread of advanced nuclear knowledge, potential new enrichment techniques, and improved weaponization and delivery capabilities could contribute to new types of challenges.

Actors of concern also have an interest in acquiring, developing, and deploying biological weapons. Global access to biotechnology capabilities and research in the life sciences are advancing at a rapid pace. These trends heighten the risk of the creation, whether through accident or design, of novel biological agents. Emerging infectious disease outbreaks and dangerous pathogen collections provide opportunities for illicit acquisition. Some endemic diseases may also present a threat if they pose an operationally significant risk to military forces. These trends will continue to challenge our national security, as well as the health of our military forces and global health security.

Attempts by adversaries to employ chemical threats, such as toxic industrial materials, create new chemical agents, and develop enhanced means of delivery will continue. The global diffusion of scientific knowledge and advanced chemical manufacturing processes may increase the chance that such efforts will succeed.

Radiological dispersal and exposure devices may become increasingly attractive to actors of concern. Although these devices do not generate the destructive effects associated with nuclear weapons, they can produce significant health, psychological, and economic effects and increase the cost of area access.

Implications for Defense Strategy and Planning

Left unchecked, these developments may destabilize the security environment. DoD policy, plans, strategy, and capabilities must be flexible to counter diverse, dynamic, and shifting WMD risks. Fiscal constraints require DoD to make strategic choices that protect and enhance countering WMD investments. The Department will accept risk in areas where WMD use is implausible, infeasible, or would have limited effects, allowing DoD to prioritize capabilities that facilitate efforts to preclude WMD acquisition and use. DoD will support other agencies and departments, rather than lead responses, to address CBRN hazards that do not typically pose an operationally significant threat, such as nuclear power plant incidents, chemical spills, and disease epidemics.

An increased emphasis on early cooperative action to shape the environment and disrupt networks has many benefits. Strategic intentions can be malleable and often reflect the security environment, presenting opportunities to dissuade actors from pursuit and possession of WMD. The dynamic structures of WMD networks can be challenging, but also offer opportunities for exploitation through flexible, innovative, and adaptive approaches targeting network hubs. These measures can help lessen acquisition incentives, bolster prevention activities, and reduce reliance on measures that carry higher political, military, and humanitarian risks. Deterrence strategies supported by credible CWMD capabilities will remain an effective approach against many WMD-armed adversaries. Recognizing that these efforts may not always be successful, DoD must also prepare a comprehensive set of capabilities to respond to WMD crises.

PRIORITY OBJECTIVES

DoD works towards the three CWMD end states—no new WMD possession, no WMD use, and minimization of WMD effects—through four priority objectives: reduce incentives to pursue, possess, and employ WMD; increase barriers to the acquisition, proliferation, and use of WMD; manage WMD risks emanating from hostile, fragile, or failed states and safe havens; and deny the effects of current and emerging WMD threats through layered, integrated defenses. These objectives define a comprehensive response to the WMD challenge and focus on shaping the environment, cooperating with partners, and prioritizing early action.

Figure 1: End States, Priority Objectives, and the WMD Challenge

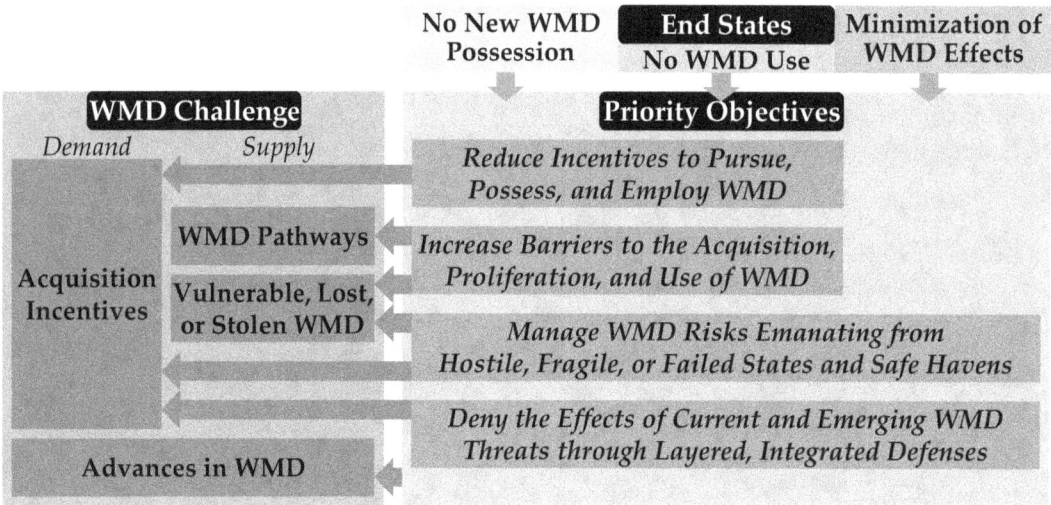

Reduce incentives to pursue, possess, and employ WMD. DoD seeks to dissuade pursuit and possession and deter the use of WMD. It does so by addressing the global and regional security drivers of acquisition, retention, and employment, supporting adherence to international treaties and enforcement of sanctions, and reducing the appeal of WMD. Through a variety of formal and informal activities, DoD also helps allies and partners that forego WMD to remain confident that their security is assured. These activities include promoting global participation in and strengthening nonproliferation regimes, providing direct security assistance, building partner capacity to counter WMD, and sustaining formal security guarantees underwritten by U.S. conventional and nuclear capabilities.

Increase barriers to the acquisition, proliferation, and use of WMD. DoD will target critical nodes and links to disrupt and defeat the acquisition, proliferation, and use of WMD. DoD will also continue to work with other departments and agencies and with international organizations and partners to secure and limit the availability of WMD-related capabilities through tailored risk reduction programs. Also critical to this objective is DoD support to negotiating, implementing, and complying with treaties, control regimes, and other multilateral activities designed to restrict the supply of WMD-related capabilities. This includes applying effective and consistent enforcement; strengthening international norms against proliferation and use; guarding against accidental or unintentional use; and securing and reducing WMD programs, stockpiles, and materials.

Manage WMD risks emanating from hostile, fragile, or failed states and safe havens. DoD must be prepared for complex WMD crises with global implications, such as the transfer of WMD or material of concern, the creation of WMD safe havens, or the threatened or actual use of WMD. The Department must also be prepared to respond to the theft or loss of control of WMD or material of concern in states that are weakly governed or under internal or external pressures. These risks present unique challenges to DoD that require adaptive or innovative operational concepts, the flexible application of military force, and the effective integration of interagency and international capabilities.

Deny the effects of current and emerging WMD threats through layered, integrated defenses. Strong defenses across a spectrum of active and passive measures that stay ahead of threat developments will help to deny adversaries the expected gains of WMD use and dissuade pursuit and possession. Effective defenses enable the Department to protect the force, project power, preserve alliances, preclude strategic gains by adversaries, and reduce risks to U.S. interests. It is particularly important to possess the ability to stop imminent WMD use and help attribute the nature and source of a WMD attack. The development and deployment of defenses must take account of both known threats and potential surprises in adversaries' WMD technology and employment methods, particularly those that could present challenges to existing countermeasures.

STRATEGIC APPROACH

The Department's approach to countering WMD is guided by the desired end states and directly supports the priority objectives. These objectives are advanced through three CWMD lines of effort: *Prevent Acquisition*, *Contain and Reduce Threats*, and *Respond to Crises*. These lines are supported by one strategic enabler, *Prepare.* Taken together, these four elements comprise DoD's approach and represent the full range of efforts undertaken by DoD to counter WMD. At any given time, DoD and its interagency and international partners will pursue multiple efforts against a broad set of actors seeking to develop, acquire, proliferate, and employ WMD.

Prepare is the continuous cycle of ensuring that the Department's capabilities support the CWMD lines of effort.

The Department will equip and train forces and develop capabilities that can be employed flexibly to shape the environment and respond to WMD threats and use. This includes efforts to provide the policy framework for CWMD activities; share information and capabilities; conduct deliberate planning; facilitate approval of operational authorities; ensure staff expertise; and sustain the Department's science and technology, research and development, and acquisition competencies. Ensuring that these preparations are adequately scoped and focused requires maintaining situational awareness of WMD activities and related capabilities globally as well as forecasting WMD threats.

DoD efforts to prepare must be embedded in the wider network of capabilities and institutions working to protect the United States against WMD threats. Partnering serves as a prudent extension of DoD's strategy and capabilities. It emphasizes building the capacity of—and interoperability with—other U.S. departments and agencies, allies and partners, and international bodies. The Department seeks to leverage and enhance, but not duplicate, capabilities resident elsewhere or activities best executed by partners.

Prevent Acquisition focuses on ensuring that those not possessing WMD do not obtain them.

DoD will continue to play an active role in reducing incentives to pursue WMD. In order to promote an international normative environment that weakens acquisition incentives and strengthens nonproliferation commitments, the Department will maximize transparency, security, and disarmament. It will also reinforce efforts to strengthen international treaties, conventions, and regimes, including the enforcement of sanctions. Equally vital is practical security cooperation focused on countering regional WMD threats. This cooperation helps partners resist incentives to acquire WMD in response to changes in their security environment. DoD will also dissuade pursuit and possession of WMD by demonstrating layered defenses built on active and passive capabilities. These measures will help convince aspirants that their activities will be detected, use attributed, and any effects mitigated. Robust defenses also contribute—in conjunction with other U.S. capabilities—to underwriting security assurances to allies and partners. They must remain confident their security is best achieved by not pursuing or possessing WMD.

DoD will continue to raise barriers to the acquisition and proliferation of WMD through pathway defeat—deliberate actions taken against actors of concern and their networks to delay, disrupt, destroy, or otherwise complicate the conceptualization, development, possession, and proliferation of WMD and related capabilities. These activities focus on the specific nodes and linkages in an adversary's WMD pathway. Pathway defeat measures are designed to create layers of complex barriers to impose recurring, collectively reinforcing, and enduring costs and setbacks on those seeking to acquire or proliferate WMD or related capabilities.

In conjunction with pathway defeat measures, DoD will also raise barriers through supporting the implementation of controls that restrict the supply of WMD-relevant materials and technologies. The Department also carries out threat reduction activities in cooperation with interagency and international partners. These efforts focus on redirecting, securing, safeguarding, and reducing at-risk WMD-related capabilities and detecting and precluding the acquisition and proliferation of WMD. DoD will also promote activities and practices that make legitimate scientific and commercial endeavors less vulnerable to misuse.

Where hostile actors persist in making significant progress toward acquiring WMD, the Department will be prepared to undertake or support kinetic and non-kinetic actions to stop such capabilities from being fully realized. DoD will manage risks emanating from fragile or failed states with WMD or related capabilities by conveying to states that proliferation undermines security and stability and working with them to enhance security. It is equally important to deny non-state actors territorial freedom of action and the means to manipulate or acquire the tools and resources of state actors.

Contain and Reduce Threats focuses on risks posed by extant WMD.

To decrease incentives for retention and employment of WMD arsenals, DoD will support the creation and implementation of effective arms control initiatives, including measures to enhance security and safety practices. The Department will also maximize transparency in its own arsenals. These efforts include the destruction and disposition of excess materials. DoD will also work to promote regional stability and to dampen destabilizing and escalatory practices and incentives.

The Department will raise barriers to WMD use by working with partners to guard against accidental or unintentional use and to strengthen international norms against the employment of WMD. Enforcing sanctions and limiting access to financial resources, materials, and commercial and military benefits can help limit the further growth of, and lower incentives to retain, WMD arsenals. DoD will also encourage and support—through direct and indirect assistance—states that secure and dispose of WMD and reduce or dismantle WMD programs.

Defenses in depth, including passive countermeasures, enhanced border security, and missile defenses, help to deter the transfer or use of WMD. As long as nuclear weapons exist, the United States will also maintain a safe, secure, and effective arsenal for deterrence purposes. Coalition operations are also a common element of contemporary military campaigns; consequently, DoD will help allies and partners develop and field integrated defenses against WMD as part of its regional military planning.

The Department will continue to develop tailored plans and capabilities to deter specific actors of concern—including those who may be serving as proxies—from employing WMD. DoD will also be prepared to lead or support operations to locate, characterize, secure, exploit, and destroy WMD. These operations may occur in a range of contingency environments and under varying security and political conditions. They will be planned and executed in collaboration with other departments and agencies as well as with international partners and organizations.

Respond to Crises focuses on activities and operations to manage and resolve complex WMD crises.

Complex crises involving WMD can arise with little or no warning and may often take place during other operations. The Department will be prepared to manage and resolve WMD crises, whether at home in support of civil authorities or abroad. These crises will require the development of flexible capabilities to respond to and mitigate risks. DoD will maintain robust situational awareness while engaging, coordinating, collaborating, and sharing information with partners.

Rapid and decisive action may be required to stop the transit and transfer of—and to recover—WMD or material of concern. In the event of loss of control, DoD will assume that hostile non-state actors who acquire WMD or material of concern will plan to use them, and act accordingly. The Department will act in coordination with partners whenever possible, but will act unilaterally if necessary. Such crises could cut across geographic areas of responsibility and require territorial containment of areas of concern as well as maritime freedom of access. These measures will assist in locating, intercepting, seizing, and securing lost or stolen items. DoD will be prepared to neutralize recovered WMD or material of concern if necessary.

DoD will also be prepared to locate, disrupt, disable, neutralize, or destroy an adversary's WMD preparations or its WMD assets through kinetic or non-kinetic operations. Layered, integrated defenses provide the means to avoid or defeat WMD attacks and mitigate their immediate effects so as to allow effective operations to continue. In response to the actual use of WMD, capabilities will be brought to bear to deny the adversary the ability to launch follow-on attacks. The Department will also provide timely technical forensics to enable strategic decision-making.

The Department will be prepared to sustain operations and support continuity of government efforts following WMD incidents. Forces and operational areas must be able to function with minimal residual limitations due to CBRN exposure or contamination. This includes not only responses to WMD use during combat operations, but also specialized activities such as those associated with CBRN installation preparedness, where force protection is critical to mission success. In addition, DoD will remain prepared to support civil authorities with CBRN response capabilities to mitigate the consequences of events in the homeland and abroad. DoD may also lead or assist in the disposal of residual adversary WMD capabilities until such time that a civilian or international entity can assume these responsibilities.

At the end of a crisis, DoD will re-establish defensive capabilities and contribute to U.S. Government efforts to restore dissuasion and deterrence. Restoring the force is critical to signaling a high degree of resiliency. These measures will demonstrate an ability to shape and adapt to the post-crisis strategic environment.

Figure 2: CWMD Ends, Ways, and Means

CWMD efforts are pursued in a continuous cycle. They are carried out simultaneously against a diverse group of actors of concern at all stages of proliferation. DoD will seek to achieve the **End States**, targeting the **Priority Objectives** via the **Strategic Approach (Ways)**, all of which are supported by **Countering WMD Activities and Tasks** (**Means**, see Figure 3). The **Means** and the **Priority Objectives** frequently span the **Ways**; for example, the primary impact of *Deny effects* is within **Respond to Crises**, but denying the effects of WMD threats also deters use within **Contain and Reduce Threats** and dissuades possession within **Prevent Acquisition**.

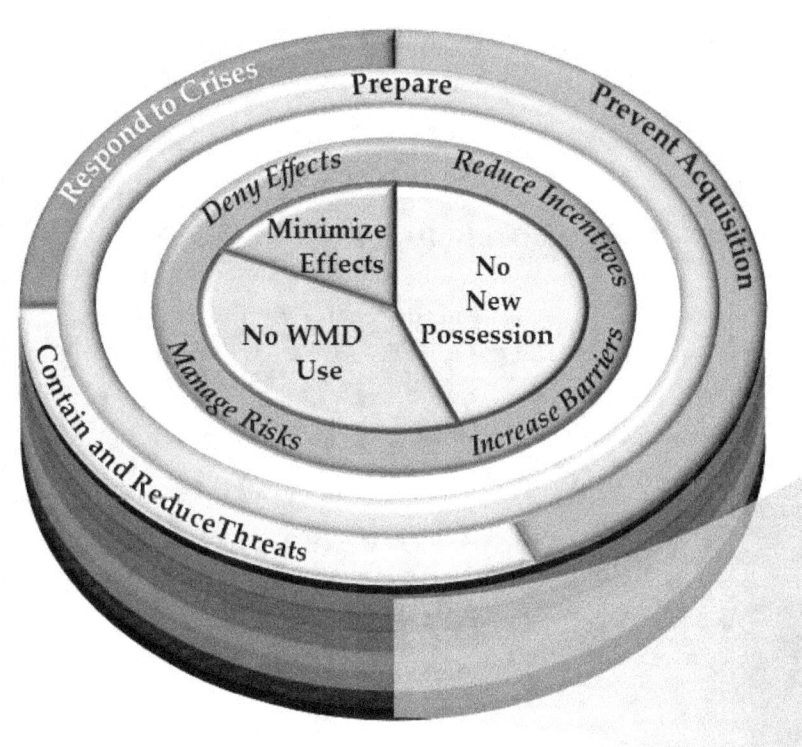

COUNTERING WMD ACTIVITIES AND TASKS

The Department will combine enabling capabilities with specialized task-oriented capabilities to counter specific WMD threats. The tasks and associated capabilities discussed below are guided by the end states, support the objectives, and are employed across all lines of effort. DoD ensures that the armed forces are prepared to counter the threat or use of WMD by a range of potential adversaries in all operational environments, including steady-state operations, lesser contingencies, and major conflicts, leading or supporting efforts as authorized.

The Department must execute three sets of activities to ensure the success of this strategy. DoD will synchronize CWMD efforts, incorporating them into broader plans and activities and leveraging enabling capabilities. DoD must also engage in foundational activities to maintain and expand technical expertise and cooperate with and support partners. These efforts in turn support specialized activities and tasks to understand the environment, threats, and vulnerabilities; control, defeat, disable, and/or dispose of WMD threats; and safeguard the force and manage the consequences of WMD use.

Figure 3: Countering WMD Activities and Tasks

Synchronizing Activities and Tasks
Incorporate CWMD Efforts & Leverage Enabling Capabilities
Integrate, Harmonize, Employ

Foundational Activities and Tasks
Maintain and Expand Technical Expertise
Recruit, Develop, Retain

Cooperate with and Support Partners
Partner, Coordinate

Specialized Activities and Tasks

Understand the Environment, Threats, and Vulnerabilities
Locate, Identify, Characterize, Assess, Attribute, Predict

Control
Isolate, Divert, Intercept, Secure, Seize

Defeat	*Disable*	*Dispose*
Delay, Disrupt, Destroy, Neutralize	Exploit, Degrade, Destroy	Reduce, Redirect, Dismantle, Monitor

Safeguard the Force and Manage Consequences
Mitigate, Sustain, Support

Any given CWMD effort will draw on capabilities in multiple specialized areas; for example, an effort under **Contain and Reduce Threats** may draw on capabilities to *locate* and *characterize*, then *isolate*, *exploit*, and *destroy* WMD; an effort to **Prevent Acquisition** could use capabilities to *locate*, then *divert*, *intercept*, or *seize* WMD-related capabilities; or an effort to **Respond to Crises** could take advantage of capabilities to *disrupt*, *destroy*, or *neutralize* imminent WMD use.

Synchronizing Activities and Tasks

Incorporate Countering WMD Efforts. Countering WMD efforts often occur as part of larger U.S. Government activities or military operations. Consequently, they must be fully integrated into other plans and activities rather than isolated as separate efforts. It is also vital to harmonize DoD activities with the efforts of other departments and agencies, state and local authorities, allies and partners, and non-governmental organizations, particularly for domestic countering WMD efforts.

Leverage Enabling Capabilities. Countering WMD efforts will employ DoD capabilities that are designed to respond to a range of other threats, meet other defense requirements, and are the responsibility of organizations with missions that extend beyond countering WMD. This includes strategic deterrence capabilities; missile defense; command and control; and intelligence, surveillance, and reconnaissance.

Foundational Activities and Tasks

Maintain and Expand Technical Expertise. DoD and its interagency and international partners rely on the intellectual capital provided by the Department's cadre of CWMD experts. DoD must nurture and sustain the knowledge and skill sets that provide the necessary expertise for countering WMD-related planning, research and development, programming, exercising, system integration, analysis, reachback, and mission execution. Maintaining expertise requires long-term activities to recruit, develop, and retain personnel. These must be reinforced with institutional support systems and education programs. To operate effectively, technical experts must train and rehearse for crisis responses and other contingencies that could occur in a variety of environments. It is equally important that senior leaders develop a strong understanding of countering WMD as an element of national security.

Cooperate with and Support Partners. Cooperation with and support of domestic and foreign security partners enhances collective, regional, and national capabilities to receive timely indicators and warnings, track material of concern, secure WMD materials and stockpiles, respond to and defeat WMD threats, and manage the consequences of attack. These efforts and capabilities promote common threat awareness, countering WMD self-sufficiency, military interoperability, military and civilian preparedness, and WMD risk reduction. Existing relationships with partners must be maintained and deepened, and new partnerships must be sought out and created. Additionally, DoD must coordinate with non-governmental organizations that can provide enhanced capabilities and capacities.

Specialized Activities and Tasks

Understand the Environment, Threats, and Vulnerabilities. It is essential for DoD to have as clear an understanding of the environment as possible. This requires creating and maintaining situational awareness of the location, quantity, and vulnerability of global materials and stockpiles and of the intentions and capabilities of actors of concern. This includes adversaries' proliferation pathways, development activities, supporting networks, decision making, and doctrine. Existing and emerging WMD threats must be located, identified, characterized, and assessed against U.S. and partner vulnerabilities, including prioritization based on risk. Additionally, the ability to attribute sources and predict threats in a timely manner is critical to support informed decision making. Finally, DoD must maintain a detailed awareness of U.S., allied, and partner CWMD capabilities and activities, incorporate this information into overall awareness, and leverage it to support the full range of CWMD efforts.

Capabilities that support these tasks include detection; modeling; detailed operational planning; and analysis of materials, precursors, and agents that may be related to a proliferation activity, an adversary's developmental or fielded capability, or the actual use of WMD. Key elements include passive and active detectors; prompt advanced diagnostics and disease detection systems; sample collection assets; responsive laboratory analysis; hazard estimation, measurement, and modeling systems; proliferation pathway analysis; and the ability to tag and track WMD materials. Sharing and integrating data from these sources are necessary to obtain a comprehensive understanding and situational awareness of CBRN threats.

Control, Defeat, Disable, and/or Dispose of WMD Threats. DoD must possess the capabilities to conduct activities to control, defeat, disable, and/or dispose of specific WMD threats. These activities will leverage capabilities to understand the environment, threats, and vulnerabilities and may draw on capabilities to safeguard the force and manage consequences. Some of these tasks may be executed with the consent and cooperation of relevant actors, but all may be required under various threat conditions and security environments across the range of military operations, and could require specialized units, equipment, and expertise.

Control activities require the ability to isolate, intercept, divert, seize, and secure WMD and related capabilities. These activities frequently occur in the steady-state, as well as within combat operations. They routinely rely on capabilities that are not traditionally considered part of the countering WMD portfolio but are nonetheless essential for success.

Pathway defeat and WMD defeat activities target the entire spectrum of an adversary's pathway from intent through development and employment of WMD. Pathway defeat activities focus on delaying, disrupting, destroying, or otherwise complicating specific nodes, links, and supporting networks prior to an adversary's acquisition of WMD. After acquisition, WMD defeat efforts target the ability to assemble, stockpile, deliver, transfer, or employ WMD. DoD will maintain and extend its ability to conduct specialized pathway and WMD defeat missions. This involves developing and fielding tailored kinetic and non-kinetic capabilities to neutralize or destroy weapons and agents; delivery systems; and materials, facilities, and processes, including the functional or structural defeat of hardened targets.

Disablement activities encompass tasks to exploit and degrade or destroy critical and at-risk components of a WMD program. These activities seek to ensure that actors of concern are unable to employ them. They also seek to reduce the risk of those capabilities being proliferated, lost, or stolen. If follow-on activities to complete WMD program dismantlement are required, WMD disablement may transition to WMD disposition.

Disposition activities seek either the partial or full dismantlement of an actor's WMD program. This includes deliberate technical processes that reduce or dismantle production methods, materials, stockpiles, and technical infrastructure; the redirection of an actor's capabilities and expertise towards peaceful productive activities; and the establishment of monitoring regimes to ensure a WMD program is not reconstituted.

Safeguard the Force and Manage Consequences. These tasks and capabilities provide the means to respond to a CBRN incident in order to mitigate hazards and the effects of use. They allow military personnel and other mission-critical personnel to sustain effective operations. They also enable support for U.S. civil authorities and foreign civil authorities as authorized. DoD must be prepared in the event that adversaries use WMD in the homeland, against allies or partners, or against deployed U.S. forces. In these scenarios, it will be essential to recover casualties rapidly, decontaminate personnel and equipment, and establish a protective posture while continually monitoring the force. Key capabilities needed to enhance force health protection include health and disease surveillance, trained and equipped forces, CBRN advisors, medical and physical countermeasures, protective equipment, platforms that provide physical protection, and decontamination systems.

TERMS AND DEFINITIONS

Unless otherwise stated, the terms and definitions contained in this glossary are for the purposes of this strategy only.

Definitions

Actors of Concern. State or non-state actors that carry out activities that, left unaddressed, pose a clear potential threat to the strategic objectives of the U.S. Government. In the WMD context, an actor of concern poses a threat of developing, acquiring, proliferating, or employing WMD, related expertise, materials, technologies, and means of delivery.

Characterize. Once a threat is identified, its external associations, internal linkages, and individual components must be determined. This includes the particular kinds of WMD and related expertise, materials, and technology that threat contains and the hazards they pose. Characterization informs assessment, attribution, and predictive analysis.

Control WMD Activities. Activities to isolate, intercept, divert, seize, and secure WMD, related expertise, materials, technologies, and means of delivery.

Countering WMD (CWMD). Efforts against actors of concern to curtail the conceptualization, development, possession, proliferation, use, and effects of WMD, related expertise, materials, technologies, and means of delivery.

Identify. Once a target is located, its nature must be analyzed to scope, categorize, and prioritize the threat it poses. Confirmation of a threat will lead to courses of action to characterize and then assess specific elements of the target more effectively.

Material of Concern. Weapons-usable CBRN material in sufficient quantity to produce a WMD or its critical components.

Neutralize. Activities to render safe mines, bombs, missiles, and booby traps or to make harmless biological or chemical agents. (Derived from JP 1-02)

Pathway Defeat. Deliberate actions against actors of concern and their networks to delay, disrupt, destroy, or otherwise complicate the conceptualization, development, possession, and proliferation of WMD, related expertise, materials, technologies, and means of delivery.

Resiliency. The ability to recover quickly and return to normal operations.

Shaping the Security Environment. In the context of countering WMD, shaping activities seek to influence state and non-state actors to eschew WMD conceptualization, development, possession, proliferation, and use.

Weapons of Mass Destruction (WMD). Chemical, biological, radiological, or nuclear weapons capable of a high order of destruction or causing mass casualties, excluding the means of transporting or propelling the weapon where such means is a separable and divisible part from the weapon. (Derived from JP 1-02)

WMD Defeat. Deliberate actions to neutralize or destroy a WMD device or agent or to prevent the device's employment.

WMD Development. The range of processes that lead to attaining WMD, including critical human resources, logistics, command and control, research efforts, production infrastructure, equipment, materials, financial networks, and other supporting networks.

WMD Pathways. Networks (links among individuals, groups, organizations, governmental entities, etc.) encompassing ideas, materials, technologies, facilities, processes, products, and events that enable actors to conceptualize, develop, possess, and proliferate WMD and related capabilities.

WMD Program. A production enterprise, regardless of size and complexity, that seeks to provide WMD to state or non-state actors. Its resources may include facilities, information, security, equipment, materials, skilled personnel, an organizational structure, and a budget. WMD programs may acquire expertise, materials, and technologies from other entities, but may also supply these to other state or non-state actors.

WMD Proliferation. The transfer of weapons of mass destruction or related materials, technology, and expertise from suppliers to state or non-state actors. (Derived from JP 1-02)

WMD-Related Capabilities. Expertise, materials, technologies, and means of delivery related to WMD.